THE LIFE OF PRAYER

The Life of Prayer

A.B. SIMPSON

CHRISTIAN PUBLICATIONS

CAMP HILL, PENNSYLVANIA

Christian Publications

3825 Hartzdale Drive, Camp Hill, PA 17011

The mark of vibrant faith

ISBN: 0-87509-419-8

LOC Catalog Card Number: 88–93030

© 1989 by Christian Publications

All rights reserved

Printed in the United States of America

96 97 98 99 00   6 5 4 3 2

Cover photo by Mike Saunier

CONTENTS

FOREWORD

I HAVE READ AND REREAD Dr. Simpson's book, *The Life of Prayer* with deepest interest and profit. No one can give this little book a careful reading without realizing that the author has lived in the secret of the Master's presence.

Every page makes it evident that here is a man whose prayers have reached God. Down through the centuries few men have had greater prayer results. Great would be the spiritual quickening if every Christian mastered this classic on the prayer life.

Jonathan Goforth

INTRODUCTION

THE LIFE OF PRAYER—great and sacred theme! It leads us into the Holy of Holies and into the secret place of the Most High. It is the very life of the Christian, and it touches the life of God Himself.

We enter the sacred chamber on our knees, stilling our thoughts with the petition, "Lord, teach us to pray. Give us Your holy desires, and let our prayer be the echo of Your will. Give us Your Spirit as our Advocate within. Open our eyes to see our Great High Priest and Advocate above. Help us to so abide in You and have Your Word so abide in us that we shall ask what we will, and it shall be done to us."

As in ignorance and weakness we venture to speak and think on this vital theme, "May the words of my mouth and the meditation of my heart be pleasing in your sight, O Lord, my Rock and my Redeemer" (Psalm 19:14). And may every true word and thought of this little volume be a living experience to him who speaks and to all who hear. So minister to the prayer life of each one, that it shall, in some measure, bring an answer to the greatest of all prayers, "Father, hallowed be your name" (Luke 11:2b).

A.B. Simpson

1

The Pattern Prayer

He said to them, "When you pray, say:

'Father,
hallowed be your name,
your kingdom come.
Give us each day our daily bread.
Forgive us our sins,
 for we also forgive everyone who sins against us.
And lead us not into temptation.' " (Luke 11:2–4)

THIS WONDERFUL PRAYER WAS DICTATED by our Lord in reply to the request from His disciples: "Lord, teach us to pray, just as John taught his disciples" (Luke 11:1). His answer was clear and simple: "Pray." This is the only way we can ever learn to pray—by just beginning to do it. The babbling child learns to speak by speaking. The lark mounts up to the heights of the sky by beating its wings again and again in the air. In like manner, prayer will teach us how to pray, and the more we pray, the more we will learn the mysteries of the heights and depths of prayer.

And the more we pray, the more we will realize the incomparable fullness and completeness of this prayer! It is unequalled by anything else, because it is the prayer of universal Christendom, the common liturgy of the church, the earliest and holiest recollection of every Christian child and the last utterance of the dying person. We who have used it most have come to feel that there is no want that it does not interpret and no holy aspiration it cannot express. There is nothing else in all the Holy Scriptures that more fully unfolds the great principles that underlie the divine philosophy of prayer.

True prayer begins in recognition of the Father

This prayer is not the cry of nature to an unknown God; it is the intelligent conversation of a child with his or her Heavenly Father. It presupposes that the suppliant has become a child and that the mediation of the Son has preceded the revelation of the Father. No one, therefore, can truly pray until he or she has received the Lord Jesus Christ as Savior and has been led into the realization of son- or daughtership in the family of God.

The Person to whom prayer is directly addressed is the Father—as distinguished from the Son and the Holy Spirit. The great purpose of Christ's mediation is to bring us to God and reveal to us the Father as our Father in reconciliation and fellowship. The title *Father* suggests the spirit of confidence, and this is essential in prayer.

The first view, then, given of God in the Lord's Prayer is not of His majesty but of His paternal love. To the listening disciples this must have been a strange expression to use as a pattern. Never had Jewish ear heard God so named, at least so named in His relation to the individual. The Father of the Nation He was sometimes called, but no sinful man or woman had ever dared to call God *his* or *her* Father. To be sure, they had heard Jesus speak of God as *His* Father. But that *they* should call Jehovah by such a name had never dawned upon their legalistic, unillumined minds.

But here Jesus is giving them a pattern to follow. They, as well as we, were to recognize God as their Father in the sense in which they were partakers of Sonship in Jesus' name. *Father* gives to prayer, from the beginning, the beautiful atmosphere of a home circle and the delightful fellowship of an affectionate, intimate friend.

Is this your pattern for prayer? Do angels marvel as they look down each day and see a humble, sinful creature of the dust talking to the majestic Sovereign of the skies like an infant prattling freely to his mother as he lies upon her breast? Could it be said to you, "I write to you, dear children, because you have known the Father" (1 John 2:13)?

Prayer should recognize the majesty and almightiness of God

The King James Version expresses the rest of the opening phrase like this: "Our Father which art in heaven." These words are intended to express God as a definite and local personality. He is not a vague influence or pantheistic presence but a distinct Person, exalted above matter and nature and having a local habitation. To Him the mind is directed where He occupies the throne of actual sovereignty over all the universe. He is also recognized as above our standpoint and level. He resides in the heavens, higher than our little world, exalted above all other elements and forces that need His controlling power. It enthrones

Him in the place of highest power, authority and glory.

True prayer must at once recognize the nearness and greatness of God. The Old Testament is full of the most sublime representation of God's majesty, and the more fully we realize His greatness, the more boldly we will dare to claim His interposition in prayer for all our trials and emergencies.

Have we learned, as we bow in prayer, that we are talking with Him who says, "I am God Almighty [El-Shaddai]" (Genesis 17:1); "I am the Lord, the God of all mankind. Is anything too hard for me?" (Jeremiah 32:26); "Do you not know? Have you not heard? He will not grow tired or weary, and his understanding no one can fathom" (Isaiah 40:28).

Prayer is a fellowship of human hearts

By addressing God as Father, each of us is lifted out of ourselves and, if nowhere else at least at the throne of grace, made to be members one of another. It is, of course, assumed that the first link in the fellowship is Christ, our Elder Brother. There is no single heart, however isolated, but who may come with this prayer in perfect truthfulness and, hand in hand with Christ, say, "Christ's and mine." But undoubtedly it refers chiefly to the fellowship of human hearts. In the Greek this is expressed as a "symphony" in prayer.

There is no place where we can love our friends more than at the throne of grace. No other exercise so fully melts away the differences of Christians and brings their hearts together in unity as prayer. There is no remedy for the divisions of Christianity but to come closer to the Father, and then we shall be in touch with each other.

Worship is the highest element of prayer

"Hallowed be your name" is the most important element of this prayer. It brings us directly to God Himself and makes His glory supreme — far above all our thoughts and wants. It reminds us that the first purpose of our prayers should always be, not the supply of our personal needs, but the worship and adoration of our God.

In the ancient feasts everything was first brought to God. Then it was given to the worshiper for his or her use. That use was hallowed by the fact that it had already been laid at Jehovah's feet. The person who can truly utter this prayer and fully enter into its meaning can receive all the other petitions of it with double blessing.

Not until we have first become satisfied with God Himself and realize that His glory is above all our desires and interests are we prepared to receive any blessing in the highest sense. When we can truly say, "Hallowed be your name whatever comes to me," we have the substance of all blessing in our hearts.

This is the innermost chamber of the Holy of Holies. No one can enter it without becoming conscious of the hallowing blessing that falls upon us and fills us with the glory that we have ascribed to Him. The sacred sense of His overshadowing, the deep and penetrating solemnity, the heavenly calm that fills the heart — these constitute a blessing above all other blessings that even this prayer can ask.

Have we learned to begin our prayer in this holy place and on this heavenly plane? Then indeed we have learned to pray!

**True prayer recognizes that establishing the king-
dom of God is the chief purpose of His divine will
and the supreme desire of every true Christian**

Christ's prayer teaches us that true prayer recognizes the establishment of the kingdom of God as the
chief purpose of the divine will and the supreme desire of every true Christian. More than for our own
temporal or spiritual needs, we are to pray for the
establishment of that kingdom. This implies that the
real remedy for all that needs prayer is the restoration
of the kingdom of God. The true cause of all human
trouble is that mankind is out of divine order. The
world is in rebellion against its rightful Sovereign.
Not until that kingdom is reestablished in every heart
and in all the world can the blessings that prayer desires be realized.

Of course it includes in a primary sense the establishment of the kingdom of God in the individual
heart, but much more in the world at large, in fulfillment of God's great purpose of redemption. In short,
the prayer is for the accomplishment of redemption
and its glorious consummation in the coming of our
Lord and the setting up of His millennial kingdom.
What an exalted view this gives to prayer! How it
raises us above our petty, selfish cares and cries!

A story is told of a devoted minister who, when
told he was dying and had only half an hour to live,
asked his attendants to raise him from his bed and put
him on his knees. He then spent the last half-hour of
his life in one ceaseless prayer for the evangelization of
the world. Truly that was a glorious place to end a life
of prayer!

Must it not be true that the failure of many of our prayers can be traced to our selfishness? Is not most of our prayer time spent upon our own interests? What have we ever asked for the kingdom of our Lord? There is no blessing so great as that which comes when our hearts are lifted out of ourselves and become one with Christ in intercession for others and for His cause. There is no joy so pure as that of taking the burden of our Master's cause on our hearts. We should bear it with Him every day in ceaseless prayer, as though its interests depended completely on the uplifting of our hands and the remembrance of our faith. "May people ever pray for him and bless him all day long" (Psalm 72:15).

Have we prayed for Jesus' petition as much as we have for our own? No ministry will bring more power and blessing on the world, and nothing will reap for us larger, eternal harvests than habitual, believing, definite, persistent prayer for the progress of Christ's kingdom! Let us pray for the needs of His church and His work, for His ministers and servants and especially for the neglected peoples who do not know how to pray for themselves. Let us awaken from our spiritual selfishness and learn the meaning of the petition, "Your kingdom come!"

True prayer is founded upon the will of God as its limitation as well as its encouragement

Real praying is not simply asking for things because we want them. The primary condition of all true prayer is the renunciation of our own will so that we may desire and receive God's will. But having done this and having recognized the will of our Father as the standard for our desires and petitions, we are to claim these petitions that are in accordance with His will, with a force and tenacity as great as the will of God itself! This petition, then, instead of being a limitation on prayer, is really a confirmation of our faith, and it gives us the right to claim that the petition thus conformed to His will shall be imperatively fulfilled.

There is no prayer so mighty, so sure, so full of blessing, as this little sentence at which so many of us have often trembled: "Your will be done." It is not the death-knell of all our happiness, but the pledge of all possible blessing! Since it is the will of God to bless us, we shall be blessed. Happy are they who suspend their desires until they know their Father's will. Then, asking according to His will, they can rise to the height of His own mighty promise: "If you remain in me and my words remain in you, ask whatever you wish, and it will be given you" (John 15:7). What better thing can we ask for ourselves and for others than that God's highest will shall be fulfilled?

How shall we know God's will? At the least, we may always know it by His Word and by His promise. We may be sure we are not transcending its infinite bounds if we ask anything that is covered by a promise of His Holy Word. Immediately we may turn that promise into an order on the Bank of Heaven and claim its fulfillment by all the power of His omnipotence and the sanctions of His faithfulness. The added phrase itself, "as it is in heaven," implies that the fulfillment of this petition would change earth into a heaven and bring glory into every one of our lives in the same measure with which we meet this lofty prayer! Therefore, while this petition implies the spirit of absolute submission, it also rises to the height of illimitable faith.

Have we understood this and learned thus to pray, "May your will be done on earth as it is in heaven?" (Luke 11:2, margin).

Prayer is trusting for every need

"Give us each day our daily bread." This gives to every child of God the right to claim a Father's supporting and providing love. It is wonderful how much spiritual blessing we get by praying and trusting for temporal needs. Some people greatly curtail the fullness of their spiritual life when they separate God's personal providence from the simple and minute interests of life and seek human provision, independent of God's interposition and care. We are to recognize every means of support and temporal link of blessing as directly from His hand. We are to commit every interest of business and life to His direction and blessing.

At the same time, it is implied that there must be in this a spirit of simplicity and daily trust. It is not the bread of future days we ask for, but bread for today. Nor is it always luxurious bread, the bread of affluence, the banquet and the feast, but *daily bread*. The best authorities translate this "sufficient bread." It may not always be bread and butter; it may be homely bread, and at times perhaps scant bread, but He can make even that to be sufficient and add such blessing with it, such impartation of His life and strength that we will know what Jesus meant in the wilderness when He said, "Man does not live on bread alone" (Luke 4:4). This implies, in short, a spirit of contentment and satisfaction with our daily lot, and a trust that leaves tomorrow's needs in His wise and faithful hands.

Have we learned to pray like this for temporal things, bringing all our life to God? Have we learned to come to Him in the spirit of daily trust and thankful contentment with our simple lot and our Father's wisdom and faithfulness?

True prayer must always recognize our need for the mercy of God

"Forgive us our sins." This is not an accidental phrase. In all honesty, we may be totally unaware of any sin in our lives. Still, there may be infinite debt, omission or shortcoming as compared with the high standard of God's holiness. The sensitive and thoroughly quickened spirit will always find there is much more to reach out for and much more that God wants to do in us.

This sense of demerit on our part throws us constantly upon the merits and righteousness of our Great High Priest. It makes our prayers forever dependent on His intercession as they are offered in His name. This enables the most unworthy to "approach the throne of grace with confidence, so that we may receive mercy and find grace to help us in our time of need" (Hebrews 4:16).

We do not mean that our Lord expects us to be constantly sinning and repenting, for the final petition of this prayer is for complete deliverance from all evil. But He graciously grades the prayer to cover every experience from that of the most sanctified to the humble but guilty penitent.

This petition presupposes a solemn spirit of forgiveness in the heart of the suppliant. This is indispensable to the acceptance of the prayer for forgiveness. The Greek construction and use of these words expresses a practical shade of meaning. The forgiveness of the injury that has been done to us has preceded *our* prayer for divine forgiveness. Freely translated, it might well read like this: "Forgive us our trespasses as we have already forgiven those who have trespassed against us."

There are certain spiritual requisites that are indispensable to acceptable prayer, even for the simplest mercies. Without them we cannot pray. The person who is filled with bitterness cannot approach God in communion. Inferentially, the person who is cherishing any other sin is likewise hindered from access to the throne of grace. This is an Old Testament truth that all the abundant grace of the New Testament has neither revoked nor weakened. "If I had cherished sin in my heart, the Lord would not have listened" (Psalm 66:18), was a lesson that even David learned from sad and solemn experience. "I will wash my hands in innocence, and go about your altar, O Lord" (Psalm 26:6). That is the eternal condition of acceptable communion with the Holy One.

The most sinful may come for mercy, but they must put away their sin and freely forgive the wrongs of others. But there seem to be two unpardonable sins. One is the sin that willfully rejects the Holy Spirit and the Savior presented by Him—the sin of willful unbelief. The other is the sin of unforgiveness.

Prayer is our true weapon and safeguard in the temptations of life

This petition, "Lead us not into temptation," undoubtedly covers the whole field of our spiritual conflicts, and we may interpret it to mean an arming against the enemies of our spirit. It cannot strictly mean that we pray to be kept from all temptation, for God Himself has said, "Blessed is the man who perseveres under trial" (James 1:12), and "Count it pure joy, my brothers, whenever you face trials of many kinds" (James 1:2). Instead, it means "So lead us that we shall not fall under temptation, or be tried above what we are able to bear."

There are spiritual trials and crises that come to people that are too hard for them to bear—snares into which many of them fall. This is the particular promise that this prayer claims: that we shall not come into any such tragic crisis; that we shall be kept out of situations that would be too trying; that we shall not be carried through places that would be too narrow.

This is what is meant by the verse, "The Lord knows how to rescue godly men from trials" (2 Peter 2:9). A still more gracious promise is given in First Corinthians 10:13: "No temptation has seized you except what is common to man. And God is faithful; he will not let you be tempted beyond what you can bear. But when you are tempted, he will also provide a way out so that you can stand under it." When you think how many there are who perish in the snare, and how narrow the path often is, there is great comfort in knowing that our Lord has authorized us to claim His protection. In these awful perils, meeting the wiles of the devil and the insidious foes against whom all our skill would be unavailing, we can stand!

This was the Master's solemn admonition to His disciples, in the garden. There, in the hour and power of darkness He urged, "Watch and pray so that you will not fall into temptation" (Matthew 26:41), and this was His own safeguard at that hour. The Apostle Paul has given us the unceasing prescription for wisdom and safety in connection with our spiritual conflict: "Pray in the Spirit on all occasions with all kinds of prayers and requests. With this in mind, be alert and always keep on praying for all the saints" (Ephesians 6:18). "Devote yourselves to prayer, being watchful and thankful" (Colossians 4:2).

The crowning petition of the Lord's Prayer is the petition for entire sanctification

"Deliver us from evil" (Luke 11:4) has been frequently translated "Deliver us from the evil one." The neuter gender, however, contradicts this and renders it to mean deliverance from evil in *all* forms. This is more satisfying to Christian experience. There are many forms of evil that do not come from the evil one. We have as much cause to pray against ourselves as against the devil. And there are physical evils covered by the petition as well as special temptations. It is a petition therefore against sin, sickness and sorrow in every form in which they could be evil.

It is a prayer for our complete deliverance from all the effects of the Fall, in spirit, soul and body. It is a prayer that echoes the fourfold gospel and the fullness of Jesus in the highest and widest measure. It teaches us that we may expect victory over the power of sin, support against the attacks of sickness, triumph over all sorrow and a life in which all things shall be only good and work together for good according to God's high purpose. Surely the prayer of the Holy Spirit for such a blessing is the best pledge of the answer! Let us not be afraid to claim it in all its fullness.

All prayer should end with praise and believing confidence

The Lord's Prayer, according to the most accurate manuscripts, really ends with "Deliver us from evil," but later copies contain the closing clause, "For yours is the kingdom and the power and the glory forever. Amen." While it is doubtful that our Lord uttered these words on that occasion, they have so grown into the phraseology of Christendom that we may, without danger, draw from them our closing lessons.

The doxology expresses the spirit of praise and consecration. We ascribe to God the authority and power to do what we have asked, giving the glory of it to His name. Then, as a token of our confidence that He will do so, we add the "Amen," which simply means, "So let it be done." It is faith ascending to the throne, humbly claiming and commanding in the name of Jesus that for which humility has petitioned. Our Lord requires this element of faith and this acknowledgment and attestation of His faithfulness as a condition of answered prayer. No prayer is complete therefore until faith has added its "Amen."

Such then are some of the principle teachings of this universal prayer. How often our lips have uttered it! Let it search our hearts and show us the imperfection, selfishness, smallness and unbelief of what we call prayer. From this day forward, let us repeat its pregnant words with deeper thoughtfulness. Let us weigh them with more solemn realization than we have done before. May they come to be to us what they indeed are: the summary of all prayer, the expression of all possible need and blessing, the language of a worship like that of the holy ranks who continually surround the throne above. Then indeed shall His kingdom come and His will be done on earth as it is in heaven!

Beautiful and blessed prayer! How it recalls the most sacred associations of life! How it follows the prodigal even in his deepest downfall and his latest moments! How it expands with the deepening spiritual life of the saint! How it wafts the latest aspirations and adorations of the departing Christians to the throne to which they are ready to wing their way.

Let it be more dear to us, more real. Let it be deeper, wider and higher as it teaches us to pray and wings our petition to the throne of grace. And if there be those who have uttered the Lord's Prayer without the right to say "Father," may they stop and think, with tears, of the lips that once taught them its tender accents years ago—lips now silent in the grave. Kneel down at the feet of that mother's God, that father's God or that sister's God. If they are willing to say, "Forgive us our sins for we also forgive everyone who sins against us," they may dare to add, linked in everlasting hope and fellowship with those that first voiced those words to them, "Father!"

On a lonely bed in a southern hospital, an old Civil War veteran lay dying. A Christian friend called on him and tried to speak about Christ, but the old man repelled him with infidel scorn. After several attempts, the Christian finally just knelt down by the bed and tenderly repeated the Lord's Prayer, slowly and solemnly. When he arose to leave, the infidel's eyes were wet with tears. He tried to brush them away and conceal his feelings, but at last he broke down. "My mother taught me that prayer more than 50 years ago," he said, "and it broke me up to hear it once again."

The Christian left, not wishing to hinder the voice of God. The next time he came to visit, the patient was not there. Sending for the nurse, he asked about the man. "He died a couple of nights ago," the nurse said, "but just before the end, I heard him repeating the words, 'Our Father, who art in heaven.' Then he seemed to add in a husky voice, 'Mother, I'm coming! He is *my* Father, too!'"

Dear friend, let this master prayer become to you a holy bond with all that is dearest on earth and a stepping stone to the gates of heaven!

Encouragements to Prayer

Then he said to them, "Suppose one of you has a friend, and he goes to him at midnight and says, 'Friend, lend me three loaves of bread, because a friend of mine on a long journey has come to me, and I have nothing to set before him.'

"Then the one inside answers, 'Don't bother me. The door is already locked, and my children are with me in bed. I can't get up and give you anything.' I tell you, though he will not get up and give him the bread because he is his friend, yet because of the man's persistence he will get up and give him as much as he needs.

"So I say to you: Ask and it will be given to you; seek and you will find; knock and the door will be opened to you. For everyone who asks receives; he who seeks finds; and to him who knocks, the door will be opened.

"Which of you fathers, if your son asks for a fish, will give him a snake instead? Or if he asks for an egg, will give him a scorpion? If you then, though you are evil, know how to give good gifts to your children, how much more will your Father in heaven give the Holy Spirit to those who ask him!" (Luke 11:5–13)

THIS IS OUR SAVIOR'S SECOND TEACHING on prayer. His first was an actual example of prayer. This is an unfolding of some special encouragements to prayer afforded by the gracious care of God. Here our Father and Friend presents deeper instructions on the nature and spirit of true prayer.

God is our Father. This was suggested by the opening words of the Lord's Prayer, but the truth is amplified in this passage by a comparison between an earthly father and our heavenly Parent. "If you then, though you are evil, know how to give good gifts to your children, how much more will your Father in heaven give the Holy Spirit to those who ask him!"

Our Father

God is a Father. How much this expresses to us! Happy is the person who can recall, in the memories of the home, the value of a father's love and care. The child, who for whatever reason, has missed that benefit, feels his or her deep need and reaches out for a father's heart and hand.

Who has not felt, especially in some great emergency, the need for wisdom and resource beyond him or herself? "Oh, if only my father were here!" Perhaps he or she has said to God, "If only You were my earthly father. Then I could sit down at Your side and explain all my perplexity. You would tell me just what to do and even do what I cannot do for myself!" His presence is as real as our earthly fathers', and we may just as freely pour out our hearts to Him, knowing that He hears and helps as no earthly father ever could!

Perhaps even better than the memory of our childhood is the realization of our own father- or motherhood. Who that has ever felt a parent's love can fail to understand this appeal? It is a love that neither the helplessness nor the worthlessness of its object can affect. It is a love that often has sacrificed everything, even itself, for the loved one. But it was from the bosom of God that all that love first came, and infinitely more is still in reserve.

The depth and length and height of this "much more" can only be measured by the distance between the infinite and the human. Much more than you love your child does He love you. Much more than you would give or sacrifice, He is ready to bestow and has already sacrificed. Much more than you can trust or ask of your father you may dare to bring to Him. Much more unerring is His wisdom, illimitable His power and inexhaustible His love! Shall we then, with our little alphabet of human experience, try to spell out all His love and learn the deeper meaning of the words, "Father in heaven"?

Our Friend

"Suppose one of you has a friend." This finds its full significance in the actual experience of each of us. Who has not had a friend, a friend who in some respects was closer than our fathers? Jonathan was more to David than Jesse was and Paul more to Timothy than his own father.

Think of how much our friends have meant to us! Recall each act and bond of love, and think of all that we may trust them for and all in which they stood by us. Put God in that place of confidence and remember He is all of that and infinitely more. Our Friend! The One who is personally interested in us; the One who has set His heart upon us. He has made Himself acquainted with us. He has come near to us in the tender and delicate intimacy of unspeakable fellowship. He has spoken to us in most gracious words, given us invaluable pledges and promises. He has done so much for us, made such priceless sacrifices and is ready to take any trouble or go to any expense to aid us.

Our Friend in trouble

More even than an earthly friend, God is a Friend in extremity. Some of us have known people who are our friends only in fair weather.

> The friends who in our sunshine live,
>   When winter comes, have flown,
> And he who has but tears to give
>   Must weep those tears alone.

But this Friend has authorized us to claim His help especially in times of need. "Call upon me in the day of trouble; I will deliver you, and you will honor me" (Psalm 50:15). "God is our refuge and strength, an ever present help in trouble" (Psalm 46:1). "I will be glad and rejoice in your love, for you saw my affliction and knew the anguish of my soul" (Psalm 31:7). That was the testimony of one who proved His faithful friendship under the severest pressure. "God . . . comforts the downcast" (2 Corinthians 7:6). "The Father of compassion and the God of all comfort" (2 Corinthians 1:3) are His chosen names and titles.

Let us not, then, be afraid to come to Him when we have nothing better to bring than our grief and fear. We shall be welcome. He is able for the hardest occasions, and He is seated on His throne for the purpose of giving help in time of need. Even if the case seems completely helpless and the hour is as dark as the midnight of this parable, cast your burden on the

Lord. Give Him all your care for "He cares for you" (1 Peter 5:7). "The Lord is close to the brokenhearted and saves those who are crushed in spirit" (Psalm 34:18).

Our Friend in unseasonable times

Our opening Scripture is a parable, comparing the man who comes to his friend at a late hour expecting a favorable reception with our Father in heaven. It was midnight and the door was shut and barred. The time for neighborly visits was long past. Nevertheless the door was opened, the petition heard and the favor granted. Whatever may be meant by the reluctance of the earthly friend to at first open the door, our heavenly Father assures us that none of these causes will prevent His hearing and helping us in the most extreme and desperate conditions or seasons. The peculiarity of God's grace is that He helps when man would refuse to do so, and its highest trophies are associated with hours when mercy seems long past and hope forever dead!

Look at King Manasseh, who for half a century was the brutal butcher of the prophets and the other saints of God. He literally fed his brutality by wrecking all that was sacred and divine. Then the hand of retribution struck him down and made him a miserable old man, captive in a foreign prison. One would think that prayer from such a man would be profanity and that all heaven would shut its ears to the idea of his escaping punishment. Yet in that late hour, Manasseh cried to the Lord. The Lord heard him and showed mercy, forgave him all his sins and even brought him again into his kingdom! Surely no person can ever say again that the hour is too late or the door too strongly barred for mercy!

Think of that city Nineveh. It was the oppressor of the nations, the proud queen of Assyria, the scourge of Israel and Judah, the boastful shrine of every abominable idolatry! Eventually its iniquities reached to heaven, and the prophet Jonah was sent to proclaim its speedy doom. "Forty more days and Nineveh will be destroyed" (Jonah 3:4). That city went to its knees—its kings, priests, princes, peasants. All were prostrated in penitential prayer! What happened? The barred gates were opened, the doors of mercy were unlocked, the terrible decree was revoked and Nineveh became a monument to the mercy of God! The children in its streets and the cattle in its stalls were specified as the objects of His tender compassion!

Consider King Hezekiah. In the fullness of his prosperity a message came from the Lord: "Put your house in order, because you will die; you will not recover" (2 Kings 2:1). Surely it looked like the closing and barring of the gates of a tomb. The sentence fell on his ears like a voice of doom. But in that hour Hezekiah prayed. A poor and trembling prayer it was, but God heard it: "I waited patiently till dawn, but like a lion he broke all my bones; day and night you made an end of me. I cried like a swift or thrush, I moaned like a mourning dove. My eyes grew weak as I looked to the heavens. I am troubled; O Lord, come to my aid!" (Isaiah 38:13–14).

Though there was little faith in that heartbroken gasp of prayer, it reached the heart of God. The stern decree that had seemed imperative and inexorable, setting up an adamant barrier to the path of life was now changing! Rather than looking through the portals of an inevitable tomb, he heard the glad words of the messenger with a gracious reprieve, "I will add fifteen years to your life" (2 Kings 20:6).

Such is the Friend to whom we pray. He stands between us and all the mighty barred doors of material force, natural law, human purpose and even divine judgment! With his hands of love He turns aside every bolt and bar that stands between us and the fullest blessing He can give our trusting and obedient hearts. Shall we ever again think anything too hard or any hour too late? He loves the hour of extremity! It is His chosen time of Almighty interposition.

Summoned to the deathbed of a little girl, Jesus took time to stop a moment while a poor, helpless woman was healed by the touch of His garment. Meanwhile the girl's life ebbed away, and human unbelief hastened to turn back the visit that was now too late. " 'Your daughter is dead,' they said. 'Why bother the teacher any more?' " (Mark 5:35). It was then that His strong and mighty love rose to its glorious height of power and victory. "Don't be afraid" was His calm reply. "Just believe."

Yes, let us go at midnight, for He that keeps Israel neither slumbers nor sleeps. Let us go when all other doors are barred and even the heavens seem brass. Remember that the gates of prayer are always open, and it is only when the sun is gone down and our pillow is but a stone in the wilderness that we behold the ladder that reaches to heaven with our infinite God at the top. Then it is that we see the provident angels ascending and descending for our help and deliverance. Jesus declared of His people that "they should always pray and not give up" (Luke 18:1).

A Friend who will not deceive us

God will never give us a stone when we ask for bread; He will give us a real and satisfying blessing. He will not give us a serpent when we come for a fish; He will never give us a harmful gift or one that contains a hidden snare of temptation or evil.

Many of the things we ask for in our blindness have serpents coiled in their folds, but He loves us too much to give us such an answer. Sometimes He must modify or refuse our petition if He would be our true Father. And we need not fear to trust this to Him. We can make the boldest requests, knowing that He who gives the greatest blessing can give the grace to keep it from being a selfish idol or a curse to our spirit. People sometimes say, "If God were to heal me or give me some temporal blessing for which I am praying, I fear it might not be best for me." Can we not trust Him for the grace as well as the gift?

"The blessing of the Lord brings wealth, and he adds no trouble to it" (Proverbs 10:22). Earthly roses fade and leave a lasting thorn. Many friendships only add to the sorrow of the parting and to the bitterness of the memory. But all that heaven gives us are everlasting joys. Let us trust Him for all we ask, and we shall have eternal cause to sing of His love and faithfulness!

This Friend gives full measure

"He will get up and give him as much as he needs" (Luke 11:8). In my Father's house there is abundant bread. Did the friend give only three loaves? No. Three were asked for, but Scripture seems to imply that he gave far more. At least he was willing to give as many as were needed. Can we not compare these three loaves to our threefold life—spirit, soul and body—and God's complete provision for it in every part? Have we claimed the ample measure? Are we satisfied today and running over with superabundant life and love for the hungry wayfarers who come to us? The man only asked for the bread as a loan, but he received it as a gift. The only return required was that of thanks and love. So our Father and Friend is ready to supply all our need "according to his glorious riches in Christ Jesus" (Philippians 4:19). Let us come, exclaiming,

> My soul, ask what thou wilt,
> Thou canst not be too bold.
> Since His own blood for thee He spilt,
> What else can He withhold?
>
> Beyond thy utmost wants,
> His power and love can bless;
> To trusting souls He loves to grant
> More than they can express.

Prayer is asking

In its simplest form, prayer is asking. "Ask and it will be given to you" (Luke 11:9). This expresses the most elementary form of prayer—the presenting of our petitions to God in the simplest terms and manner. We are undoubtedly taught that even the most ordinary and imperfect request that is sincerely presented at the throne of grace receives the attention and response of our Heavenly Father. The infant's helpless cry reaches the mother's heart the same way the young believer's feeblest gasp reaches the heart of God.

Prayer is waiting upon God

There is a higher form of prayer, though. "Seek and you will find." This denotes the prayer that waits upon God until it receives an answer. Then, having received the answer, this one follows up that answer in obedience to His direction until it finds all it seeks, whether light or health or strength from on high. It is the prayer that listens to the Lord, watches daily at His doors, waits at His doorway (Proverbs 8:34). "Let us press on to acknowledge him" (Hosea 6:3).

Prayer is more than asking — it is receiving, waiting and learning of Him. It is a converse and a communion in which He has much to say and we have much to learn. This is the prayer that has so often brought us His peace, His heavenly baptism of love and power, His blessed working out of the problems of life. "To you, O Lord, I lift up my soul; in you I trust, O my God. Do not let me be put to shame" (Psalm 25:1–2). "Those who seek the Lord lack no good thing" (Psalm 34:10). Prayer is not asking for things as much as it is a seeking for God Himself and pressing into that fellowship that is beyond all other gifts. This is that which carries with it every other needed blessing!

Prayer is overcoming

Then there is prayer for which the promise is given, "Knock and the door will be opened to you" (Luke 11:9). This is more than seeking. Prayers of this kind surmount the great obstacles of life, the closed doors of circumstances, the gates of brass and the unyeilding mountains of hindrance and opposition. These prayers, in the name of our ascended Lord and in the fellowship of His mediatorial rights and powers, press through every obstacle and tread down every adversary! It is not to be thought of as prayer that knocks at the gates of heaven and extorts an answer from an unwilling God. No, it is the prayer that carries forth the promise and the answer against the gates of the enemy and beats them down, just as the walls of Jericho fell before the tramping and shouting of Israel's believing hosts!

This is the prayer that takes it place at the side of our ascended Lord, claiming what He has promised to give, even commanding in His mighty name. It is faith dipping its hand into the omnipotence of God and using it in fellowship with Him until His mighty name prevails against all that opposes His will, until the crooked things are made straight, until the gates of brass are opened and the fetters of iron are broken asunder!

Such prayer is seen as Moses stands on the mount with God while Joshua fights in the plain below. There he stands, holding up the hands of victorious faith, seeing the hosts of Joshua keep step with his uplifted hands. The battle advances or ebbs as those hands go up and down, but eventually they wave high over a victorious field. There Moses built an altar and proclaimed the memorial name, Jehovah-Nissi — "The Lord is my Banner" (Exodus 17:15). That name has become our watchword from generation to generation ever since it was declared: "The Lord will be at war against the Amalekites from generation to generation" (Exodus 17:16). It is when our hand is upon the throne of the Lord that He wages war with our enemies, and they fall before His victorious will!

Such prayer can also be seen in Deborah, kneeling in her tent that day when Barak led the host of Israel against the legions of Sisera. In her great heart she was feeling the surging tides of that terrible warfare, knowing by the throbs of her faith and prayer when the battle waxed or waned. But she had fought it all over on the field of vision, and as she claimed the last victorious onset and commanded the last foe to flee in Jehovah's name, her exulting spirit shouted in the victory of faith! Although her eyes may not have seen the battlefield, her spirit cried out, "March on, my soul; be strong!" (Judges 5:21).

Her soul had trodden down the foe. Her spirit had triumphed in the conscious power of Jehovah. Her faith had knocked at the gates of the enemy until the impossible wall was laid in the dust and brazen gates were shivered into fragments and scattered as by the whirlwinds of the sky. This is what is meant in James 5:16 — "The prayer of a righteous man is powerful and effective."

Prayer is persistent

We are instructed to come in the spirit of boldness and importunity. "Because of the man's persistence he will get up and give him as much as he needs" (Luke 11:8). This is a difficult passage — one that has been interpreted in various ways. Some have tried to show that "persistence" means "extremity." They say the man was heard because of his extreme distress, not because of his persistence. I cannot agree with this view.

The Greek word literally means "without shamefacedness." It is the negative form of the word shamefacedness that occurs in First Timothy 2:9, and it properly means boldness and audacity. There is nothing whatsoever unscriptural in this. Indeed, it is constantly reiterated in the New Testament that we are to come boldly and with confidence to the throne of grace (Hebrews 4:16). We are to claim our redemption rights in all their fullness. "In him and through faith in him, we may approach God with freedom and confidence" (Ephesians 3:12). "Therefore brothers . . . we have confidence to enter the Most Holy Place by the blood of Jesus . . . let us draw near to God with a sincere heart in full assurance of faith" (Hebrews 10:19, 22).

There is no doubt that if Esther had hesitated to enter into the presence of the king at the crisis of her country's fate, she would have lost her blessing and at the same time risked the fortunes of her nation. If modest Ruth had feared to claim her lawful rights at the feet of Boaz under the law of the kinsman, she probably never would have been his bride nor the mother of the long and honored line of kings from David to Jesus.

There is no doubt but what our frightened unbelief and our shrinking timidity have lost us many a redemption right. But a bold and victorious confidence that claims its inheritance in the name of our risen and ascended Lord is pleasing to God. That is the meaning and teaching of this beautiful parable—we are to come freely to our Father and Friend, no matter what doors seem to be closed or what discouragements may frown across our way.

Someone has said that the secret of success in human affairs has often been audacity. There is a holy audacity in Christian life and faith that is not inconsistent with the profoundest humility. And in that holy audacity lies the secret of the victorious achievements of a Moses, a Joshua, an Elijah and a Daniel in the Old Testament. In the New Testament there is the Syro-Phonecian woman and the glorious apostle of faith. Likewise there are the Luthers and Careys who have pioneered gospel truth and missionary triumph in the Christian dispensation.

Prayer considers others

Perhaps the highest ministry of prayer is that which is offered for others. The petition of our Scripture was not for the suppliant himself but for a friend who had come to him after a long journey. The literal meaning is that this was a friend "who had lost his way."

It suggests the needs of those for whom we should constantly come to our heavenly Friend. It is of this that the Apostle James says in referring to prayer: "Confess your sins to each other and pray for each other so that you may be healed. The prayer of a righteous man is powerful and effective." Then he adds, "My brothers, if one of you should wander from the truth and someone should bring him back, remember this: Whoever turns a sinner away from his error will save him from death and cover a multitude of sins" (James 5:16–20).

Thank God, we can bring to Him those people who have lost their way — unsaved friends, wandering sons and daughters, other Christians who have forsaken their first love and the blessedness they knew when they first saw the Lord. He will not refuse to hear their cry or fail to give them the living Bread!

Often our boldest prayers will be those we pray for others. For ourselves we may fear a selfish motive, but for them we know it is a prayer of love. And if it be the prayer that seeks His glory, we can claim for it His mighty and prevailing will and intercession. If you have felt your way closed for service, this is a ministry that all can exercise, and it is the mightiest ministry of life! Let us be encouraged, from this day forward, to use it in fellowship with Him who has spent the centuries that have passed since His ascension in praying for others. This is the work of our Great High Priest before the throne!

Prayer and the Holy Spirit

The last lesson about prayer this passage teaches is that the Holy Spirit is the source and substance of everything prayer can ask for. He is the Gift who carries with Him the pledge of all other gifts and blessings.

"How much more will your Father in heaven give the Holy Spirit to those who ask him!" (Luke 11:13). This is spoken as if there was really nothing else for which we should ask. It is still more remarkable that in the parallel passage in Matthew 7:11, the language used is, "How much more will your Father in heaven give good gifts to those who ask him!" So then, the Holy Spirit and "good things" are synonymous. A person who has the Holy Spirit shall have all good things.

Was not that the symbolic meaning of the widow's oil in the ancient miracle (2 Kings 4)? Her pot of oil poured into all the empty vessels became sufficient to pay all her debts and furnish an income for all her future life. All she needed was the pot of oil; it was the currency for every blessing. So is the Holy Spirit. The person who has this heavenly gift is in touch with the throne of infinite grace and the God of infinite fullness, and there is nothing that he or she cannot claim! When shall we learn to seek first the kingdom of God and His righteousness, and know that all these things shall be added to us?

Our Father "out" of heaven

Let me call your attention to a beautiful Greek construction in the closing verse that refers to our Heavenly Father. The expression here should read, "your Father *out* of heaven," in contrast to "our Father *in* heaven" as given in the Lord's Prayer earlier in the chapter. Why this blessed and stupendous change? Because in the later passage, our Father has already begun to move toward us, to enter our hearts by the Holy Spirit whom He has just sent to make a heaven below for every praying heart. So while we begin the prayer with our eyes directed upward, we end it with our inmost being filled with the presence and fullness of God and with the rich blessing of His abiding grace and power!

What a blessed heavenly altar of incense, standing by the rent veil, wafting its sweet fragrance into the outer and inner chambers! Let us be found there,

> Where heaven comes down our souls to greet;
> And glory crowns the Mercy Seat.

In His Name

In that day you will no longer ask me anything. I tell you the truth, my Father will give you whatever you ask in my name. Until now you have not asked for anything in my name. Ask and you will receive, and your joy will be complete.

Though I have been speaking figuratively, a time is coming when I will no longer use this kind of language but will tell you plainly about my Father. In that day you will ask in my name. I am not saying that I will ask the Father on your behalf. No, the Father himself loves you because you have loved me and have believed that I came from God. (John 16:23–27)

"FOR JESUS' SAKE" AND "IN JESUS' NAME" are phrases familiar to every ear in Christendom. Yet as we glance at their deeper meaning, we will probably find that these phrases are used with little understanding. This is the profound teaching about prayer that the Master emphasizes in His closing addresses to His disciples.

God as revealed in Jesus Christ

"Whatever you ask in my name" might be translated, "Whatever you ask the Father as represented by me." It expresses Christ's identity with the Father.

The Father had been known to Jews by many different names: *Elohim* (as in Genesis 1:1), the God of nature; *El Shaddai* (as in Genesis 17:1), the God of power; *Adonai* (as in Genesis 15:2), the God of providence; *Jehovah (as in Genesis 4:16),* the God of covenant grace. But now He is to be known as Jehovah-Jesus meaning God in Christ. This is undoubtedly implied in the language of this passage and involved in the thought to which the Savior is giving expression. It is the same thought that He repeats in the parallel verse, "I will do whatever you ask in my name, so that the Son may bring glory to the Father" (John 14:14). There it plainly expresses that the Father and the Son are acting in perfect concert. Furthermore, it is only through the Son that the Father is glorified and revealed to man or understood by him.

The idea may be carried so far as to do away with the distinct personality of the Father and the Son, and this of course would be extreme and erroneous. But keeping this in mind and recognizing fully the dual personality, it is true that the Father Himself is revealed to us in the person of the Son. We are to present our petitions to the Father and feel encouraged to expect His gracious answer because of what we know of Jesus, through whose presence and teachings God has become revealed to us.

As we would come with confidence to our Savior, let us come with the same confidence to His Father, for "Anyone who has seen me has seen the Father" (John 14:9). The words that He spoke were given by the Father who dwelt in Him. The love that He manifested was the Father's love, whom He came to reveal. He is the brightness of His Father's glory, the express image of His person and the reflection of His will and character. It is to God in Christ, therefore, that we are to pray. Let us, then, learn to pray in the name of Jesus.

Mediation and intercession

We know God because we know Jesus, and we can come to Him only because of Jesus, our Mediator. There are deep necessities for this in the nature of God and the relationships of sinful men with Him. So deeply did Job realize this that he cried out for a daysman or mediator. "If only there were someone to arbitrate between us, to lay his hand upon us both" (Job 9:33). His cry was for some being that could touch at once both heaven and earth and bring them into harmony and fellowship.

This is just what Christ has done! His incarnation has bridged the infinite gulf between the eternal, spiritual Deity and finite man. Jesus in His death has united sinners with their offended God, praying "Father, forgive them for they do no know what they are doing" (Luke 23:34), and appealing to sinful men, "Be reconciled to God" (2 Corinthians 5:20).

Not only has Christ brought God and men into reconciliation and fellowship, but He keeps that fellowship unbroken by His ceaseless intercession. "He always lives to intercede for [us]," therefore "He is able to save completely those who come to God through him" (Hebrews 7:25).

This idea of mediation is widely illustrated in the Holy Scriptures. We see it in the story of Joseph and his relationship to Pharaoh and the Egyptians. "Go to Joseph" (Genesis 41:55) was the king's response to all who came to him for relief or for judgment. All the affairs of the kingdom were entrusted to his administration, and he was the mediator and channel of all communication.

We see this truth again in the beautiful story of Esther as she ventured to touch the golden scepter and stand between her people and their oppressor and danger. By her courage and patriotism she saved her nation from extinction.

Still more impressively was this truth foreshadowed in the ministry of Moses who became, at Sinai, the channel of communication between God and the terrified people. "Speak to us yourself and we will listen," was their cry. "But do not have God speak to us or we will die" (Exodus 20:19). And God consented to use Moses as the channel of His revelations to Israel and to teach the lesson of our Great Mediator.

But the most striking of all the ancient types of Christ was Aaron, the Hebrew High Priest. It was his special office to stand between the people and God and present their worship in the Holy of Holies and make intercession for their sins and needs. For them he passed through the open veil, stood beneath the Shekinah, presented the blood and incense at the mercy seat and came back to them with the benediction of Jehovah. In all this he was but the type of a better ministry of the Great High Priest, Jesus Christ, in the true Tabernacle of heaven. There He has entered with His own blood, through the veil of His own flesh, and now appears in the presence of God for us.

The ministry of Aaron may well express the deeper meaning of Christ's High Priesthood. Upon his heart the ancient priest continually carried, engraved in precious jewels, the names of Israel's tribes. Our Great High Priest perpetually carries our names on His heart, permanently engraved and worn as jewels of ornament and pride amid all the glories of the heavenly world.

This does not just mean that on special occasions He prays for us and takes our petitions to His Father. Undoubtedly He does, but He continually prays for us, even when we are too ignorant or too forgetful to pray for ourselves. Every moment He holds our names before His Father in unforgetting love and ceaseless remembrance!

Aaron not only carried the names upon his heart, he carried them upon his shoulders. Even so, upon the strong arms of His omnipotence, our ascended Lord continually bears our burdens, as strong to help as He is swift to hear.

The ancient priest bore upon his brow a beautiful and significant symbol, a coronet with jeweled letters, carrying the significant words, "Holy to the Lord" (Exodus 28:36–38). This he was to bear continually as he entered the Holy Place, that he might bear the iniquities of the children of Israel. So, too, our blessed Intercessor bears upon His brow this inscription, not for Himself, for His holiness is never questioned, but as the proclamation of our holiness and perfect acceptance. He covers the imperfection of our holiest service with His perfect righteousness and keeps us constantly accepted in the presence of holy angels and the infinite and heart-searching God.

What infinite meaning these figures give to the simple words, "In his name"! How wide they open the gates of prayer, and how perfect the consolation they give to the timid heart! "Therefore, since we have a great high priest who has gone through the heavens, Jesus the Son of God, . . . Let us then approach the throne of grace with confidence, so that we may re-

ceive mercy and find grace to help us in our time of
need" (Hebrews 4:14–16).

Grounded on the finished work of Christ

His intercession for us is based upon His sufferings
and His blood. The cross is its foundation. The accomplished redemption He claims for us was purchased by His blood, and by it we receive the promises of the everlasting covenant.

There is a story of a seasoned soldier who often
pled for the pardon of his brother, also a military man
but an unruly and undisciplined one. This man had
been convicted on several occasions of desertion, but
his brother's words always saved him from execution.
The man, however, would not change his nature. At
last the kind general declared that in the interests of
public order, the next offense would have to be followed by the full penalty. It would be useless to plead
any more. Another offense did come, and the sentence
at the court-martial was about to be pronounced
when the general saw the brave soldier weeping si-
lently in the ranks. When asked if he had anything to
say for his brother, the old veteran simply stood and
quietly raised the stump of his amputated arm. Words
were useless now, but tears coursed down his cheeks
and many around him wept as they thought of all it
meant of sacrifice and devotion to his country.

That was all his plea. Holding up the pledge of his
sufferings and love pled more eloquently than any
speech could ever have done. And eloquently it did
plead, for with tears of emotion, the old commander
answered, "Sit down, my brave fellow. You shall have
your brother's life. He is unworthy of it, but you have
purchased it by your blood."

In like manner our Redeemer pleads for us. He does not beg for mercy that would be simply gratuitous and unbought. No, He boldly asks for that which is His purchased right and for that which His own blood has been sacrificed. Long before the incarnation and the cross, He had entered into a covenant with the Father. There by His immutable oath, God had made a great promise: If Christ would bear the sins of men and pay for all the penalties of the holy law, He would receive as His mediatorial right forgiveness for every penitent and believing sinner who would accept His gospel and all the resources of His grace. Now, He simply claims His redemption rights and our rights through Him by virtue of that promise.

Asking in Jesus' name therefore is asking that for which Jesus has suffered and died and that which He has freely and fully purchased for all His own. Surely with such a plea, we may come boldly to the throne of grace and ask as much as the precious blood of Calvary is worthy to claim. How much that is, it will take all eternity to tell!

The strong ground of our prayer for salvation is that salvation has been purchased and that forgiveness is the birthright of every believing penitent. This too is the plea of our prayer for sanctification, for "by one sacrifice he has made perfect forever those who are being made holy" (Hebrews 10:14). This is the foundation likewise of our plea for physical healing, for "He took up our infirmities and carried our diseases" (Matthew 8:17) and purchased redemption for our suffering bodies. And on this ground we may claim every other needed blessing, for "He who did not spare his own Son, but gave him up for us all—how will he not also, along with him, graciously give us all things?" (Romans 8:32).

Have we learned the significance of His name and the power of His cross and blood as the strong and all-prevailing plea of the believing suppliant at the throne of grace?

Our identity with Jesus

"In his name" expresses our relationship with Him as well as His relationship with the Father. It means in His person, in His stead, on His account, as if the petitioners were the Son Himself! All of us know something of how far a human name and introduction will go. The friend we introduce in our name is received in some sense as we would be received. Still more is this the case when he or she is commended to us on the ground of a special relationship with the one we love. The wife is received by her husband's family as if she were a part of him and kin with them. In his name she comes to them as he would come.

In the days that followed the Civil War, many an incident was told of the special bonds that grew between fellow soldiers. They were bonds of fellowship and suffering on the battlefield or in the hospital. One such story was told of a tramp that called at a farmhouse one afternoon. The housewife was rather alarmed and suspicious, but the stranger took from his well-worn pocket a scrap of paper and handed it to the woman. It was the writing of her own son! It told how this man had fought by his side and then had nursed him in the hospital until the last hour had come. Now as these lines were being written, he was committing this last message to his family into the hands of this friend. The son asked, for his sake and in his name, that they receive the man and love him as he, the son, had been loved.

That was enough! The haggard face, the ragged clothing and the tramplike appearance of the stranger were all forgotten. The rough man was clasped in the arms of that father and mother and taken into that family circle as their own child, for the sake of another!

In this same way we become identified with our Savior. Our Heavenly Father receives us in Jesus' name as He receives Him. This is what faith may claim as it comes in Jesus' name. We enter into His rights, we ask on His account and we expect to be welcomed and loved even as He is loved! This was our Savior's bequest to us in His intercessory prayer found in John 17. "Let the world know that you sent me and have loved them even as you have loved me" and "that the love you have for me may be in them and that I myself may be in them" (verses 23 and 26). Are we too bold if we claim that which He Himself has asked for us as our place and privilege and right?

Not only may we claim His rights, but we must also come in His will and spirit, and ask what He Himself would ask. The privilege is limited by its nature. We cannot ask in the behalf of Christ what Christ Himself would not ask if He were praying. "In his name" therefore means we are praying in harmony with His will and at the prompting of His Spirit. We may not, therefore, claim from God that which would be sinful or selfish, or involve harm to another, or hindrance to the cause of Christ.

All our asking must be within this eternal limit: "Your will be done on earth as it is in heaven" (Matthew 6:10). But this will is larger than we could ever comprehend. Within this large and ample place there is room for every reasonable petition for spirit, soul and body, for family, friends, temporal circumstances, spiritual services and the utmost possibilities of human desire, hope or blessing.

Finally, this identity with Him implies that He will be in us as the spirit of faith, making it His prayer and supplying the spirit and conditions of effectual, prevailing intercession!

Such then is the divinely appointed channel of prayer. How it encourages the unworthy and weak to come to the mercy seat with full assurance of faith! You may be a poor sinner, but He who represents you in heaven is the righteousness of God. On His brow, above your name, He carries the flashing jeweled coronet that inscribes you standing in Him: "Holy to the Lord."

You may be an obscure and insignificant disciple, but He who endorses your petition has the mightiest name in earth and heaven! You may be a timid spirit and a fainthearted child of unbelief and fear, but there is One who bids you have the faith of God, who offers Himself to you as the spirit of faith and prevailing prayer. This is the One who said, "Father, I thank you that you have heard me" (John 11:41), and "Father, I want those you have given to me to be with me where I am, and to see my glory" (John 17:24). Now in His faith you may claim with boldness all His will, and go forth in deepest humility, yet with sublimest confidence, saying

> I am not skilled to understand
>   What God hath willed, what God hath
>   planned,

But this I know, at His right hand
Stands One who is my Savior.

CHAPTER

4

The Prayer of Faith

"Have faith in God," Jesus answered. "I tell you the truth, if anyone says to this mountain, 'Go, throw yourself into the sea,' and does not doubt in his heart but believes that what he says will happen, it will be done for him. Therefore I tell you, whatever you ask for in prayer, believe that you have received it, and it will be yours" (Mark 11:22–24).

THERE IS AN UNSEEN PRINCIPLE OF FORCE in the material world that is more powerful than all the physical elements we touch or see. It is the force of attraction that holds the physical universe together. Not only does it hold in cohesion the minutest particles of matter, it is the cause by which, in a sense, all things consist or hang together. But for this cohesive force, our bodies would dissipate into impalpable air, the raindrops and the oceans would dissolve into vapor, the mountains would crumble to pieces and the great world itself would explode in a catastrophe of wreck and dissolution.

In its wider application, it is the force that holds our planet in its orbit and keeps it on course during its awesome journey of more than 500 million miles a year. Without this special power controlling it, earth would rush into the distant fields of immensity. Because of this power, our world follows its unmarked

55

path amidst the spheres without diverging a hair-breadth from its course.

And it is the same power that holds other planets and systems on their special tracks. What is this force? Gravity! It is completely unseen and noiseless. There is no vibration in its mighty heartthrobs, no reverberation from its voice, no trace of its viewless but mighty arm. Yet this power is greater than the earth, which it poises in space and propels along its pathway. It is mightier than the sun, which sweeps the circle of the solar system with its revolving circuit of planets. Mightier it is than all the stars in all their spheres. Think of the great, invisible, intangible, inaudible, impalpable secret of the material universe and all its mighty movements. How simple is this subtle force, and yet how sufficient and sublime!

Ascending from the material world to the social, rational and human sphere, we find a corresponding principle that holds society together like gravity holds the universe. What is it that binds the family together, that cements the friendships of life, that controls the partnerships of business and leads men continually to stake their whole fortune on their investments and securities?

What is it? Confidence, trust, faith between people! Without it, the home circles would be torn with strife and wrecked with distrust and misery. Without it, political and national fabrics would collapse and government would be impossible. Without it, business would be ruined. Not a single bank could stand a day without the trust of its constituents, and no security would be of any worth if people stopped trusting the promises and reliability of each other. The world has even adopted the word "trust" for the names of some of its strongest institutions. There must be some fascination in the term, and well there should be, for trust is the law of gravity for the social world.

Let us carry this thought to its true plane and apply it to the great spiritual kingdom, of which all natural things are but imperfect types. Would it seem strange if this law of faith were found to be the principle of the spiritual world as it is of the natural — the underlying force that holds it together, the remedial principle that is to bring back our own lost orb to its true place in the circle of the heavens? Such indeed it is!

Faith is the essential principle of the kingdom of God. It was loss of faith that first separated man from God. The fall of the race began the moment Adam and Eve listened to Satan's insinuations, "Did God really say . . . ?" (Genesis 3:1). The recovery of the race commences the moment people begin to trust God. That is why faith has been made indispensable to the reception of the gospel and salvation. This is why it is forever true, "Whoever believes in him is not condemned, but whoever does not believe stands condemned already because he has not believed in the name of God's one and only Son" (John 3:18). Faith is the gateway to salvation, and it is not strange that it should be made the gateway of prayer.

Faith is necessary to effective prayer

Our Lord makes this clear. He commands the disciples to have faith in God, and then adds, "Believe that you have received it, and it will be yours" (Mark 11:24). We are told in Hebrews 11:6 that "without faith it is impossible to please God, because anyone who comes to him must believe that he exists and that he rewards those who earnestly seek him." There must be a believing recognition of God's personal existence, of His goodness and graciousness and of the fact that He hears and answers prayer.

The prayer of faith is linked to healing: "the prayer offered in faith will make the sick person well; the Lord will raise him up" (James 5:15). If we would understand what James meant by "the prayer offered in faith," we have only to turn to the first chapter and hear him say,

> If any of you lacks wisdom, he should ask God, who gives generously to all without finding fault, and it will be given to him. But when he asks, he must believe and not doubt, because he who doubts is like a wave of the sea, blown and tossed by the wind. That man should not think he will receive anything from the Lord. (James 1:5-7)

This is emphatic language. Of course God will give to all, but they must take by faith what God gives or the giving is in vain. The man who wavers does not take and therefore cannot receive. Such are the people to whom the Lord offers the Water of Life but fail to drink it.

There are prayers that God has answered, but we do not enjoy the answers. There are persons whom God has long ago forgiven but they continue on in darkness and despair because they did not trust His pardon. When the troubled and despairing father came to Jesus with his epileptic child, he wept, "Lord, have mercy on my son. I brought him to your disciples, but they could not heal him." Upon hearing this, the Master demanded of His disciples, "How long shall I stay with you? How long shall I put up with you? Bring the boy here to me." Then "Jesus rebuked the demon, and it came out of the boy, and he was healed from that moment." When they were alone, Jesus told his disciples, "If you have faith as small as a mustard seed . . . nothing will be impossible for you" (Matthew 17:16–21).

It is perfectly right that God should require us to believe before He answers our prayers, because faith is the law of the New Testament and of the gospel dispensation. The Apostle Paul speaks of two laws in the fourth chapter of Romans: the law of works and the law of faith. The former has been superseded and the latter is the principle on which the whole gospel is based.

"To the man who does not work but trusts God who justifies the wicked, his faith is credited as righteousness" (Romans 4:5). We have already suggested why this law has been adopted. No doubt in the light of eternity, we shall find many reasons for it, which we could not now fully comprehend. But it is enough to know that it was through unbelief that men fell, so it is through faith that they must be restored. In a word, we must come back to that point from which we all started in the wrong direction.

When Bunyan's pilgrim found he had lost his roll on the Hill of Difficulty, he simply went back to the place where he had lost it and started on again. And so must we begin once more at the point of departure from God—by learning to trust Him. God is bound to act upon this principle, and He cannot justly acknowledge our plea if we do not present it according to the prescribed rule.

If this is true, as it surely is, it works in both directions. While on the one side it is gloriously certain that "According to your faith it will be done to you" (Matthew 9:29), so the other is just as certain: "According to your unbelief it shall *not* be done to you." It may be that God, for His consistency, is required to keep His word to those who doubt Him as well as to those who believe Him. Otherwise the enemy of souls might accuse Him of falsehood and inconsistency for answering prayers of unbelief!

Our Lord has announced this as the principle of His throne of grace, the law on which petitions will receive attention and consideration. Surely we cannot afford to disregard this sacred intimation or venture into His presence expecting our unbelieving, compliant and insulting doubts and insincerities to bring any blessing from His hand.

Faith is the mighty force in the spiritual world

Faith is not only the law of the Christian dispensation; it is also a mighty force in the spiritual world. The act of believing God for anything He has promised is, in reality, a creative force that produces effects and operations of the most important character! Indeed it seems that faith is the principle upon which God Himself acts, the secret of His power in creating matter and in commanding the events of providence. "He spoke and it came to be; he commanded, and it stood firm" (Psalm 33:9). When the disciples wondered at the withering of the fig tree, Jesus simply said it was an act of divine faith. It was the faith of God that produced it, and he commanded them to "have faith in God" (Mark 11:22).

The faith of God must mean the faith that God Himself exercises. In Romans 4 we are told a little about this faith of God. We read that Abraham acted like Him "who gives life to the dead and calls things that are not as though they were" (Romans 4:17). God commands that which is not and expects it. He believes in the efficacy of His own command without a shadow of hesitation. Therefore He sees it instantly and ultimately accomplished. Even for the things that lie in the future in His purpose, He counts them as if they were present or past. The lapse of time is nothing in His mind and involves no uncertainty as to the results.

Our Lord so believes in the things that are not that He calls them by names of actual realities. Long before Abram even had a child, God told him plainly, "I have made you a father of many nations" (Genesis 17:5). Jesus Christ is spoken of as "the Lamb that was slain from the creation of the world" (Revelation 13:8). The cross was as real to the Father ages ago as it is now. He speaks of you and me as if we were already sitting in the heavenly places, shining like the sun in the kingdom of our Father.

It was this faith in Jesus Christ that commanded and compelled the quickening of Lazarus in his tomb. It was a resistless force, a divine power that actually moved upon second causes and compelled their obedience. If that faith of God is in us, it will be a corresponding force, and there will be in us that effective, working prayer that accomplishes much! At the moment we are offering it and believing God for its answer, God is moving upon some heart and making that one conscious of His presence and power.

Surely this is reason enough for us to pray in faith. It is a spiritual force that God requires us to cooperate with, to enter into, to use with Him and for His glory. The mighty forces of nature must have man's cooperation or they are lost and wasted. Electricity goes to waste if we do not constrain it to our will and use it according to its own laws. Even so, by our faith we must take hold of God's omnipotence and actually use it, with deep humility but also with holy confidence, for the carrying through of His own great purposes!

Looking into the invisible world

If only we could see behind the curtains of the invisible world, we would be able to trace living streams of spiritual power passing from the heavens at the instant the prayer of faith ascends from our lonely place of prayer. There we would see that prayer of ours reach out instantly and touch the persons whose names are being held up before the throne. Two streams of heavenly power would be distinctly visible: one, an ascending line from us as we kneel in supplication, and the other, a descending current of power upon some far-distant heart.

Such phenomena have actually been traced in innumerable instances. While Elijah was praying on Carmel, the clouds were actually marshaling on the distant horizon. While Jacob prayed at Peniel, the heart of Esau, as he lay in his tent that night, was going back to early memories and melting into the tender welcome that he gave the following noon to his once-hated brother. While holding up special mission fields in far distant lands, Christians have found that at that moment, showers of blessing have descended. While some weeping wife or mother has been praying for her husband or son, those hearts were being converted hundreds of miles away!

Faith is a power as mighty as that which we see when we touch the electric switch or open the valve of the engine or turn the control that ignites the dynamite under a mountain of rock! When God requires us to pray in faith, then, He is simply requiring us to join hands with Him in the exercise of His own almighty power and be partakers of His mighty working!

Faith is essential to our own spiritual welfare

The faith God requires of us in prayer is essential to our own spiritual welfare. Even if it added no direct ulterior result in the actual answer, it would be abundantly repaid in the blessing that believing prayer brings to our own spirits. How it quiets our fears, tranquilizes our agitation and stills our troubled spirit! It enables us to submit to God and say, "Your will be done on earth as it is in heaven" (Matthew 6:10). We will never choose this until we believe that His will for us is only love and blessing.

So wonderful are the subjective benefits of prayer that many go so far as to say that they comprise all the value of prayer. This would be a foolish conclusion to reach, for it would be a strange blessing if we were only comforted by an imaginary dream, with no objective reality. Take away the actual reality of God and the facts of prayer, and you take away the foundation of our subjective comfort. If God is not real and the answer not actual, then our comfort is a lie and our ulterior peace is a delusion. But if we know God is real and that His promise will actually be fulfilled, then we can rest our troubled heads upon His breast and our hearts upon His promises. We can be still and know that He is God.

How self-possessed and restful are those who have learned to trust God for all they ask! How sweetly these two thoughts are combined in the gracious words of the apostle in Philippians: "Do not be anxious about anything, but in everything, by prayer and petition, with thanksgiving, present your requests to God. And the peace of God, which transcends all understanding, will guard your hearts and your minds in Christ Jesus" (4:6–7). Here we have the injunction to pray about everything — without care, doubt or anxiety. After that follows the promise that the peace of God will keep our hearts and minds through Jesus Christ.

God requires our trust

But God requires our trust in order to keep us from hindering His answer to our prayer by our own restless activity or flight. When we ask God to do something for us, we must give Him time to do it. While He is working, we must be careful to avoid rushing off in unbelieving haste to do something that might hinder His plan. If God were to come with the answer to our prayer, He would no doubt find many of us absent. We had long since fled in fear, first firing our gun as a sentinel might do and then running off as fast as possible.

Suppose Israel had not believed God when they cried to Him at the Red Sea. If they had rushed back toward their foes or forward into the deep or up into the mountains where God had made no promise of showing His power, what would have happened? His promise was to divide the sea! To prevent their running in panic, He had to command them through Moses, "Do not be afraid. Stand firm and you will see the deliverance the Lord will bring today" (Exodus 14:13). Afterward they were commanded to "move on" (verse 15) in His way and claim their freedom.

If Joshua's hosts had not believed God and marched around Jericho at His command, they would never have found the answer that was awaiting their seventh circuit on the seventh day. Much later, we find the prophet Isaiah pleading with his people to be quiet and not hinder the deliverance that they had asked God to give them from Sennacherib and his army. But instead of this, they insisted upon doing something to help themselves; they sent an embassy into Egypt for an alliance with Pharaoh. The prophet tried to warn them that the Egyptians would not be able to help them; their strength was to sit still. "In repentance and rest is your salvation, in quietness and trust is your strength" (Isaiah 30:15). Their reply? "No, we will flee on horses" (verse 16). Even after that, God mercifully warned them that their "pursuers will be swift!" Then the prophet added, "Yet the Lord longs (KJV, waits) to be gracious to you. . . . Blessed are all who wait for him!" (verse 18).

In due time they found out that their Egyptian alliance was of no help. Furious that they would try such a thing, Sennacherib returned with a fierce and cruel scorn, bidding his caged prisoners to prepare for their doom. With no one else to rely on, Hezekiah prayed to the Lord. Not until then did God send an angel at night, who swept along the line of Syrian tents, bringing death to all the attacking army! It was totally without any contriving on Israel's part. That next morning saw an army of corpses, and the seiged city found itself gloriously free! (Isaiah 37)

God requires us to trust Him and be still until He brings His answer to us and works it out in our lives. Without faith we are sure to do something to hinder

Him or get out of the place where we can receive the answer in its fullness.

Believing for what we cannot see

Is it reasonable to believe for an answer that we do not yet see? How can we believe for that which we do not know or see to be actually so? Simply because, if we did see and know from other evidence, it would not be believing at all, but learning from the evidence of our senses. We believe only when we do not see. "Faith is being sure of what we hope for and certain of what we do not see" (Hebrews 11:1). God's way for us is to believe first, on the simple evidence of His promise, and to continue to believe without other evidence until we have proved our faith without sight. Then He will permit us to see and know by the demonstration of the fact itself.

This is nothing more than what we are doing every day in the affairs of human life. Millions of dollars are invested in our commercial exchanges every week on the simple faith of a phone call or an item of news in the daily paper. Values are bought and sold on paper where the actual realities have not been seen by either party. Securities are constantly negotiated by those who buy them on simple trust. It is humiliating to think that we cannot put the same confidence in the Word of God!

Likewise, we are in the habit of recognizing things as done when in fact they are only decided; long weeks and even months must go by before we see their actual accomplishment. A friend of mine had a disability application pending. It meant everything to him and his family: on one side was a life of possible poverty; on the other was comfort and provision.

There was considerable delay and uncertainty, but at last the message of approval came. I suppose we could say that it was really not true, because the family had not yet received the first check. In one sense, we might be right, because they would not actually receive a check for several months. But would that really make a difference? No! Long before the family had the money, arrangements were made for the future months as calmly as if they had just finished depositing the first check in the bank. To them, the official notice was enough, and they could truthfully say, even in the face of a critic, "We have our disability compensation!" They had all that was necessary to make it certain.

In like manner, the moment our petition passes the throne, we are justified in believing that we have exactly what we have asked for, and we can say, "I have received my answer, praise the Lord!"

This was what God intended to teach Daniel when He sent the angel from heaven. Daniel had been praying for 21 days, and the angel said to him, "As soon as you began to pray, an answer was given" (Daniel 9:23). "Do not be afraid, Daniel. Since the first day that you set your mind to gain understanding and to humble yourself before your God, your words were heard, and I have come in response to them. But the prince of the Persian kingdom resisted me twenty-one days" (Daniel 10:12).

From the beginning when his prayer raced toward heaven, Daniel was justified in counting the answer as given. But the delivery of the blessing and even the message was hindered by the opposition of the enemy. Nevertheless, all the opposition of earth and hell cannot stop God's purposes! To His mind and to the mind of faith, they are as certain from the start as they are when they take as vivid a form as the solid mountains and become the facts and memories of actual life!

The difference between faith and hope

All God's promises to His children are gauged on this pattern. To the penitent sinner Christ's word was instant and final: "Your faith has saved you; go in peace" (Luke 7:50). To the disciples His message of cleansing was, "You are already clean because of the word I have spoken to you" (John 15:3). To the sick and suffering the decree also went forth, "Be clean" (Matthew 8:3); "Receive your sight" (Luke 18:42); "Your request is granted" (Matthew 15:28); "Your son will live" (John 4:50); "According to your faith will it be done to you" (Matthew 9:29).

To Abraham the word that carried with it all the promises of the future was in the perfect tense: "I have made you a father of many nations" (Genesis 17:5). The explanation of this was given in Romans 4:17. "God . . . calls things that are not as though they were." It is the basic principle of His divine government, yet it is the one thing from which so many shrink back. It is the essence of all true faith, and the lack of it shows clearly the line of demarcation between effective faith and that which is only hope.

In light of all this, should we not rise to something higher than the mere reasonings of probability? Can we not get above mere hope and encouragements? To a degree, these can be obtained even without God. Is not God's Word more dependable that all our feelings, all the endorsements of men or even all the actual evidences of its fulfillment? Even those evidences may not last long, "but the word of our God stands forever" (Isaiah 40:8), and "not the least stroke of a pen, will by any means disappear from the Law until everything is accomplished" (Matthew 5:18).

Be deliberate in prayer

Let us learn to be deliberate in our prayers. Many people pour out a reckless mass of ill-considered supplications much like a child blowing bubbles into the air, scarcely expecting to ever see them again.

The habit of asking indiscriminately wears out the power of believing. It is a pity to ever ask anything from God that we have to abandon and confess to be of no significance. To take the name of our God in vain is a serious thing, and everything asked in His name without meaning or effect is of this character. Every time we find our prayers ineffective, we are weakened for our next attempt. After a while, like iron heated and cooled successively over and over, the temper of our faith is worn out.

If we would ever learn the prayer of faith, we must learn to pray with thoughtful deliberation, carefully weighing our words before the Lord as He has weighted His promises, for "the words of the Lord are flawless, like silver refined in a furnace" (Psalm 12:6). The secret of faith is always to endeavor to ascertain, before we pray, whether we are asking according to God's will. Then we can take the simple stand of John: "This is the assurance we have in approaching God: that if we ask anything according to his will, he hears us. And if we know that he hears us—whatever we ask—we know that we have what we asked of him" (1 John 5:14-15).

Let us cultivate the habit of so believing when we have prayed. Let us commit the matter to God and recognize it from then on as one of the things He has promised and agreed upon. Then it becomes a thing for which we cannot pray again in the sense of an unsettled question. Faith is a matter of definite will, at least to a certain extent. We must choose to believe, and then fix our will as a sailor sets his helm. God will swell our sails and hold our helm for us in the attitude in which we have set it. We cannot create the faith, but we can choose to believe, and God will sustain us in our choice and uphold us in our trust!

Claiming the faith of God

We must claim the faith of God, letting the Spirit of Jesus sustain our faith with His strong faith. We must choose to believe, and then He will enable us to claim His promises. This follows consistently, of course, with the whole doctrine of Christ's indwelling life. We must trust Him for our faith as well as for our love and holiness. But in each case, we must yield ourselves and choose to stand in the position assumed, throwing ourselves upon Him to sustain us. This He will do, baptizing us with such a spirit of prayer and confidence that we shall be empowered to claim and humbly command the blessing that He has already decreed.

After this we must stand firm and not be shaken by either delay or apparent denial, drawing comfort and encouragement even from His seeming refusals. Then, at last, our Lord will look upon us as He did the Syro-Phoenician woman, with admiring love, and say, "You have great faith! Your request is granted" (Matthew 15:28).

Let us realize that God is preparing us for higher destinies and placing upon us each day heavier loads of discipline. Thus we may be trained for the mightier activities of faith we are to share with our Lord in the eternal world. Let us not stagger under these loads. Let us be like Abraham of old who "did not waver through unbelief regarding the promise of God, but was strengthened in his faith and gave glory to God, being fully persuaded that God had power to do what he had promised" (Romans 4:20–21). Then we shall find that "our light and momentary troubles are achieving for us an eternal glory that far outweighs them all" (2 Corinthians 4:17).

Hindrances to Prayer

So that nothing will hinder your prayers (1 Peter 3:7).

As the goal of a good relationship between a Christian husband and his believing wife, Peter places the value of unhindered prayer.

The greatest hindrance to the life of prayer is sin. "Surely the arm of the Lord is not too short to save, nor is his ear too dull to hear. But your iniquities have separated you from your God; your sins have hidden his face from you, so that he will not hear" (Isaiah 59:1-2).

God would rather let Israel be defeated at Ai and go into captivity to Babylon—in spite of the possible prayers of a Joshua, Noah, Daniel or Job—if the answering of these prayers would have countenanced the sin of His people (see Ezekiel 14:12-14). Yes, even that beautiful and consecrated temple must be reduced to rubble and the name of Jehovah dishonored by His enemies, rather than have sin sanctioned by a holy God.

David admitted, "If I had cherished sin in my heart,/ the Lord would not have listened;/ but God has surely listened/ and heard my voice in prayer" (Psalm 66:18). The Apostle John adds his testimony to this heart-searching truth when he tells us that "if our hearts do not condemn us, we have confidence before God and receive from him anything we ask, because we obey his commands and do what pleases him" (1 John 3:21–22).

Saints around the altar were praying for an old farmer who wanted to have peace with God. Eventually he got up and said God would never answer their prayers "as long as that ox is in the wrong stall." He hurried away and returned his neighbor's property. The next night he came back with shining face and a light heart and testified that the blessing came the moment he put the hindrance away.

God can hear the prayers of sinners. Otherwise none of us could have access to the throne of grace. But it is a different matter when we are deliberately committing sin. This is the coolest insolence and presumption in the face of heaven. When sin is confessed and put away, though, the Lord will freely bless. But while we stand with evil conscience and wrong intent, expecting God to overlook our disobedience and presumption, we can only accept the same awful message He gave to the leaders of Israel who came and sat down before the prophet Ezekiel.

> Son of man, these men have set up idols in their hearts, and put wicked stumbling blocks before their faces. Should I let them inquire of me at all? Therefore speak to them and tell them, "This is what the Sovereign Lord says: When any Israelite sets up idols in his heart and puts a wicked stumbling block before his face and then goes to a prophet, I the Lord will answer him myself in keeping with his idolatry. . . .

Repent! Turn from your idols and renounce all your detestable practices! . . .

When any Israelite or alien living in Israel separates himself from me and sets up idols in his heart and puts a wicked stumbling block before his face and then goes to a prophet to inquire of me, I the Lord will answer him myself. I will set my face against that man and make him an example and a byword. I will cut him off from my people. Then you will know that I am the Lord" (Ezekiel 14:2–8).

This is frequently the cause of long-unanswered prayer and the reason why God's people fail to enter into the fullness of blessing they seek. God is searching their hearts and bringing to their remembrance long-forgotten sins that He wants them to deal with.

Suppose we are at some secret crisis of life: perhaps seeking entire sanctification, the baptism of the Holy Spirit, healing from some alarming disease, salvation for some precious friend or deliverance in some great emergency. God will search the heart and bring to our conscience things long forgotten. He will enable us to search and try our ways and lay open our hearts before Him in repentance. Only then may we receive His blessing, unhindered and unbounded, and know the blessedness of the man "whose transgressions are forgiven,/ whose sins are covered./ Blessed is the man/ . . . in whose spirit is no deceit" (Psalm 32:1–2).

Let us, then, search and try our ways and turn again to the Lord. Let us be willing to say, "Search me, O God, and know my heart;/ test me and know my anxious thoughts./ See if there is any offensive way in me,/ and lead me in the way everlasting" (Psalm

139:23–24). Then no sin can hinder our prayers or our perfect blessing. The valley of Achor will become the door of hope, and the place of forgiven sin and self-crucifixion will be marked as the starting point of a new and higher life of usefulness.

Selfishness and earthly desire hinder prayer

"When you ask, you do not receive, because you ask with wrong motives, that you may spend what you get on your pleasures" (James 4:3). God cannot give us all the things that our carnal nature clamors for anymore than we would give our child the gleaming knife he or she sees on the kitchen counter. These things would often be more dangerous to us than the keen edge of the knife would be to the child.

Many "good" things can be desired from an earthly and selfish motive and in a carnal spirit. Many people seek forgiveness to escape the remorse of a guilty conscience—and so that they may continue on in their godless selfishness. Most people who have no true sense of honor are quite willing to be accepted as candidates for heaven if God will let them enjoy the pleasures of the world on their way. Prayer for healing may be simply an expression of the desire to get free from pain and be able to enjoy the pleasures of life.

Things that God in other circumstances would be quite willing to give us, He often has to refuse us because they would separate us from Him. At a later period in our lives, we find Him able and willing to give us the same things without reserve, because in the meantime we have been able to lay them all on the altar to be used for His glory and in union with Himself.

That is why the Lord's Prayer, as we have already

seen, begins with prostration of our whole being at the feet of God: "Hallowed be your name,/ your kingdom come,/ your will be done" (Matthew 6:9–10). We cannot be trusted to ask anything for ourselves until our spirit is thus consecrated to God.

This is the meaning of the profound promise of Psalm 37:4: "Delight yourself in the Lord/ and he will give you the desires of your heart." The heart that has found its joy in God cannot desire anything that God cannot grant. First He gives it proper desires and then their fulfillment.

Is it not true that many unanswered prayers have been thoroughly selfish ones? Have those longings for our spiritual good been prompted either by fear or self-love? Have not those prayers for the salvation of your children and friends been as selfish as your desire to see them well settled in life? Have we shown as much desire in petitioning God for the children of others? It is our right that we should seek these blessings for ourselves and for our own, but if the spirit is to be a true spirit of prayer and union with God, there will be some higher motivation than selfish or human love and desire.

Strife and bitterness are a hindrance to prayer

"When you stand praying," our Savior said to His disciples, "if you hold anything against anyone, forgive him" (Mark 11:25). "In your hearts do not think evil of each other" (Zechariah 7:10). That was the message of the prophet Zechariah to the people of the Restoration, as he taught them the secret of God's blessing in their trials.

One reason why the disciples could not claim the casting out of the demon from a suffering child was that they had earlier disputed as to which of them would be the greatest in heaven. The spirit of cherished animosity, lurking prejudice, sullen vindictiveness or cold disdain will as effectively obstruct our communion and intimacy with heaven as a speck on the crystalline lens of the eye will obstruct our vision. It only takes the crossing of some small electrical wires to shut down the machines and leave a building in total darkness!

There are many "crossed wires" in the church of Christ, and the consequences are darkened hearts and mournful cries. "Has God forgotten to be merciful?" (Psalm 77:9). "O Lord God Almighty,/ how long will your anger smolder/ against the prayers of your people?" (Psalm 80:4). "How long, O Lord, must I call for help,/ but you do not listen?" (Habakkuk 1:2). Just this long: "If you are offering your gift at the altar and there remember that your brother has something against you, leave your gift there in front of the altar. First go and be reconciled to your brother; then come and offer your gift" (Matthew 5:23).

The spirit of prayer is essentially a spirit of love. Frequently when we are at some crisis of prayer and much is hanging upon God's answer—perhaps life itself or something more precious than life—we find ourselves confronted with just such a test as this. Someone will be remembered whom we once were at odds with, and somehow we just could not forgive that one. Let us remember in that hour that we cannot hurt another by our irritation or retaliation as much as we can deeply wound ourselves and hinder the blessing of God. In the presence of infinite love, no breath of hate can live one moment.

He prayeth best who loveth best,
   All things both great and small;
For the dear God who loveth us,
   He made and loveth all.

Samuel Taylor Coleridge

It is especially with respect to this matter of love that John speaks about our heart condemning us in prayer. Above all other things, it is perhaps that which we are most likely to overlook and that which God is least likely to pass by.

Is this hindering your prayers? Can you think of any person from whom you are wrongly estranged — some person whom you treat with studied harshness, neglect, disdain, injury or injustice? Is there some word you have spoken against another that you should not have spoken, even if true? Have you heard some word against your brother to which you should not have listened? May God help you to discover and deal with any such cause of unanswered prayer!

Doubt is a hindrance to prayer

"He who doubts is like a wave of the sea, blown and tossed by the wind. That man should not think he will receive anything from the Lord" (James 1:6–7). This is strong language, but there is no question that the sin of unbelief, from the divine standpoint, is the most damaging of all spiritual conditions. It destroys the contact of the soul with God as effectively as the cutting of a telephone line would terminate a conversation.

We have already seen that the word *receive* in this passage of James means to *take*, and it denotes two things: God's anger with unbelief, because He gives "generously to all without finding fault" (James 1:5); and mankind's inability to take what God gives. That is, his doubt shuts up all his spiritual sensibilities and capacities and renders him incapable of absorbing and appropriating the blessing that is offered at that time.

God holds us responsible for our doubt, yet He does not require us to produce, by our own will, the faith that brings us into His love and blessing. This is His gift to us. He does require us, though, to prevent it from running out, as from a leaking vessel, through the openings of miserable doubts. There is one thing we can do — we can refuse to doubt! We can refuse to entertain the questioning and fear, the morbid apprehension and subtle satanic insinuations. If we do this, God will do the rest, enabling us to stand fast in faith and press forward to the fullness of His blessing!

This is where the enemy concentrates his strongest attacks. He waits for the hour of the trial, when our prayer seems to be refused and delayed. Then he begins hurling his shafts of evil suggestion into our trembling hearts, trying to drive us from our confidence and to betray our own cause by consenting to his wicked questionings. But Christ has said, "I tell you the truth, if anyone says to this mountain, 'Go throw yourself into the sea,' and does not doubt in his heart but believes that what he says will happen, it will be done for him" (Mark 11:23). Even Abraham "did not waver through unbelief regarding the promise of God, but was strengthened in his faith and gave glory to God" (Romans 4:20).

In like manner we are to hold fast to the faith we have professed, for "God [has] power to do what he [has] promised" (Romans 4:21). "My righteous one will live by faith. And if he shrinks back, I will not be pleased with him" (Hebrews 10:38). God waits to give His blessing to the soldiers who stand their ground and who, when the blessing comes, are there to claim it.

Perhaps you say, "I have already doubted and forfeited my blessing. Is it too late to receive the answer?" No, not if you repent of your doubt as you would of any other sin, and immediately bring forth fruits of repentance by refusing from then on to be beguiled by the same sin. Often we find that such a fall thoroughly convinces people of the sinfulness of doubting and cures them of falling into it thereafter.

Have you been trifling with God in this matter of prayer and defrauding yourself of the blessings for which you have already suffered so much? May the Lord set your face like a flint, fix your feet on the rock and stay your spirit upon God!

Ignoring God's will hinders prayer

It is not necessary for actual sin to be present in our lives to hinder prayer; it may simply be plain disobedience to the Spirit's voice in some definite leading to service or testimony. I have known many people who did not receive the full answers to their prayers for the baptism of the Holy Spirit until they had obeyed the voice of God in some particular where they had been shrinking or hesitating. Others have failed to receive the answer to their prayer for healing because they were standing in some forbidden place. Some were holding back their testimony for God out of fear. Others lost out by failing to take some step of faith to which the Holy Spirit was calling. It was not until after months and even years of striving with God that they learned the lesson. Then after prompt and thorough obedience, they received perfect deliverance and wonderful blessing.

The Bible gives some solemn examples of good men who stood on forbidden ground and found their power and defense departing from them. The mighty Samson lost his hold upon God the moment he forfeited separation and let his hair be cut. Abraham had no power while in a compromising attitude in Egypt. Jacob had no vision of God during the years of his wandering. Even Josiah lost his heavenly protection and sacrificed his life because he stepped beyond the divine will of God. He went unbidden against Pharaoh Necho, king of Egypt, even after being warned of his fate if he persisted in his rash presumption. Any of us could lose our stand with God if we persistently disobey His call to special service or if we press forward where He has said, "No."

It is a serious matter for those who are walking in the Spirit to trifle with God's voice or to be disobedient to His commands. Such disobedience may interrupt all communication with Him and hinder all prayer.

Forbidden methods can be a hindrance to prayer

It is possible to ask God's help in a proper manner and spirit, and then immediately go to work to help Him fulfill that prayer in an unlawful manner. No doubt Jacob sincerely asked God for the coveted blessing. But he then proceeded to take the most unworthy means of accomplishing that purpose, thus involving himself in years of waiting and sorrow. Unquestionably, Moses was sincere when he asked God to deliver Israel by His hand, but he proceeded in the most rash and improper manner to accomplish his patriotic desire, by slaying an Egyptian. Thus he involved himself in crime and peril.

Abraham surely thought his compromise with Hagar was going to assist God in giving him that promised son. But his actions only silenced the heavenly voice and brought upon himself domestic strife and trouble. Worst of all, it hindered the object he had at heart!

Certainly Saul of Tarsus sincerely prayed for salvation for many a year, but he sought it by his own righteousness. He missed his aim by not submitting himself to the righteousness of God. In like manner, his whole race today is praying in vain for mercy, yet rejecting God's only appointed way to receive it.

Many pray for sanctification, but they fail to enter into the blessing because they do not intelligently understand and believingly accept God's appointed means to achieve it. Prayers for the salvation of others are often hindered because the one who prays for his or her friend takes the wrong course to bring about the answer.

I knew a woman who was pleading for her husband's salvation. She hoped to win him over by avoiding anything that might offend him. She yielded to his worldly tastes in the vain hope of attracting him to Christ. Her efforts would have accomplished far more if her attitude had been one of fidelity to God and fearless testimony for Him. That God could bless!

When we ask God for a blessing, we must allow Him to direct the steps that are to bring the answer. He will give His power to everyone who will let Him hold the reins. Many invalids are praying for healing, yet directly neglecting God's prescription for the disease. They resort to means He has not countenanced and would probably forbid, especially to one who claims to be in the attitude of simple faith. God's answer must be brought by His own messengers, and the steps that we take in bringing about the answer must be based on His absolute direction!

Take the course of David, the second time the Philistines invaded his realm after his coronation. Suppose David had done just what he had done before and marched directly against them without first asking God to bless him. He would have been defeated. This time the command was entirely different from the previous occasion. God told him, "Do not go straight up, but circle around behind them and attack them in front of the balsam trees. As soon as you hear the sound of marching in the tops of the balsam trees, move quickly because that will mean the Lord has gone out in front of you to strike the Philistine army" (2 Samuel 5:24). Here we see that the answer was dependent upon explicit obedience to the Lord's directions.

Is this not the reason why many of our prayers go unanswered? Have we waited for our Master's orders and sought the answer in the direction He indicated? How solemn are the words of the prophet Zechariah: "This will happen if you diligently obey the Lord your God" (Zechariah 6:15). It is like an echo of God's word concerning Abraham: "I have chosen him, so that he will direct his children and his household after him to keep the way of the Lord by doing what is right and just, so that the Lord will bring about for Abraham what he has promised him" (Genesis 18:19).

Ignorance of the Holy Spirit is a great hindrance

For many Christians, prayer is little more than a cry for help in a time of despair or pain. It is like the cry of a suffering brute or the wail of an unconscious infant. True, God hears the faithless cry of human misery, but this is not prayer. The voice that continually reaches the Father's ear is that of His trusting child who prays with the breath and power of the Holy Spirit Himself. True prayer should be by His prompting, and it is because most people know Him so little and walk with Him at such a distance that they are comparative strangers to the language of heavenly communion.

The life of prayer is an interior life, a spiritual life. Many people do not realize this, and many actually do not want it. It holds too constant a check on the heart. It requires too completely that they walk with our God. People like to be their own masters. The habit of walking step by step with God, submitting every thought and desire to an inward Monitor is intolerable to their imperious will. At the least, it is unfamiliar to their experience.

But this is the key to the life of prayer. It is an interior life. Its home is "in the shelter of the Most High" resting always "in the shadow of the Almighty" (Psalm 91:1). It is constant, intimate fellowship—a divine companionship. It is Enoch walking with God. It is Elisha clinging to his master and saying, "As surely as the Lord lives and as you live, I will not leave you" (2 Kings 2:2). It is the breath of the inner man, and it is as necessary as the beating of our hearts and the breathing of our lungs!

This is the difficulty with much of our prayer—it is a spasmodic cry of emergency rather than the habitual fellowship and conversation of a heavenly life. If you were accustomed to walking close by His side, you would not want to get far from Him and have to call loudly in the hour of extremity. It is the habit of constant prayer that prepares you for the great conflicts of prayer. If you neglect the little, you will find yourself unprepared for the big emergencies. God is calling you to a closer walk with Himself. He is asking you to open your heart for His continual abiding, to receive the Spirit of grace and supplication. He wants to become to you the strong One who will inspire all your petitions and bear them on the wings of His love and power to the Advocate on high. Then, through Him, you will receive from the Father the answers to the prayers He inspires!

If you possess the Holy Spirit in your heart, you have a private connection to the throne of God. At any moment, day or night, you can open and maintain direct communications with heaven, bringing all its help, if need be, to your immediate aid! Surely it is worth your while to yield yourself to a consecrated life and allow your loving Lord to make your heart His temple and His throne. Then prayer will ever be the familiar and unbroken line of a happy child with the Father who is always at hand!

Our ready supply

Happy are those who are thus within continual reach of the full supply for every need and balm for every wound! Sorrow may overshadow, Satan may assail, difficulty may encompass, but through prayer, relief is always ready and the spirit always victorious. From every conflict, the inner self returns fresh and strong. Phoenixlike, it rises from its own ashes and grows with each renewing in freshness and gladness.

A South American traveler tells of a curious conflict that he once witnessed between a weasel and a large poisonous snake. The little creature seemed no match for its antagonist, which threatened to destroy it and its helpless brood. Still it fearlessly faced the strong enemy and, rushing directly toward the snake, struck it with a succession of fierce and telling blows. The snake retaliated with what appeared to be a fatal strike, and for a moment it looked as if the struggle was over.

But the wise little creature retreated into the jungle and found a plantain tree. Eagerly it devoured a portion of its leaves, then immediately returned to the fight with fresh vigor and determination. Again and again this spectacle was repeated: the serpent ferociously attacked and the animal would run to the tree, strengthening itself and returning to fight with new power. When it was all over, the giant snake lay dead. The little victor was unharmed in the midst of the nest with its offspring. They survived what appeared to be instant destruction.

How often we are wounded by Satan's sting—wounded, it would seem, to death! If we had to go through some long ceremony to reach the source of life, we would faint and die. But, thank God, there is forever a Plant of Healing. He is as near to us as that nourishing tree of the jungle, and to Him we may continually retreat and come back refreshed and invigorated like Him who, as He prayed on the mount, shone with the brightness of celestial light! As Jesus prayed in the garden, He arose triumphant over the fear of death. He was strengthened from on high to accomplish the mighty battle for our redemption!

The victories of prayer!

The victories of prayer are the mountaintops of the Bible. They take us back to the plains of Mamre, to the fords of Peniel, to the prison of Joseph, to the triumphs of Moses, to the victories of Joshua, to the deliverances of David and to the miracles of Elijah and Elisha. The victories of prayer take us back to the whole story of the Master's life, to the secret of Pentecost, to the keynote of Paul's unparalleled ministry, to the lives of saints and the deaths of martyrs, to all that is most sacred and sweet in the history of the church and the experience of God's children.

Some day the last conflict will have passed, and the footstool of prayer will have given place to the harp of praise. The scenes of earth that will be gilded most with eternal radiance will be those often linked with deepest sorrow and darkest night. Then, over it all, we may read the inscription: "Jehovah-Shamma—the Lord was there!" Only that which God touched shall be remembered or be worth remembering forever. These will be imperishable memorials. From this day forward may they cover every pathway and every step of life's journey! And may we recognize that whatever comes is but another call to prayer and another opportunity for God to manifest His glory and to erect an everlasting memorial of His victorious love!

I began and now I end this book with the fact that the Master taught His disciples to pray by starting them at once to pray. Begin then this moment to pray for the first thing that comes to your heart as a need. Then go on turning everything into prayer until you have to stop because of the fullness of praise in your heart.

And "now to him who is able to do immeasurably more that all we ask or imagine, according to his power that is at work within us, to him be glory in the church and in Christ Jesus throughout all generations, for ever and ever! Amen" (Ephesians 3:20).